Finance for Thought, for the Teenager

Kathleen Hiebert

iUniverse, Inc.
New York   Bloomington

iUniverse books may be ordered through booksellers or by contacting:

iUniverse
1663 Liberty Drive
Bloomington, IN 47403
www.iuniverse.com
1-800-Authors (1-800-288-4677)

Because of the dynamic nature of the Internet, any Web addresses or links contained in this book may have changed since publication and may no longer be valid. The views expressed in this work are solely those of the author and do not necessarily reflect the views of the publisher, and the publisher hereby disclaims any responsibility for them.

ISBN: 978-1-4401-4817-0 (sc)
ISBN: 978-1-4401-4818-7 (ebook)

Library of Congress Control Number: 2009930729

Printed in the United States of America

iUniverse rev. date: 10/02/2009

Contents

Introduction

I have wanted to write this book for about fifteen years, not only for the benefit of my little brother, my nephews, my nieces, and my daughter, Alex, but also for all the other kids out there who haven't had anyone take the time to explain some basics of money management.

Given the current condition of the economy, it has never been more apparent that one of our biggest failures has been the lack of teaching money management. We need to inform our teenagers and teach them independence—not dependence. Money and finance are some of our most valuable subjects to understand, but yet underrated. I wish these subjects were a prerequisite for high school graduation.

It is important to understand the basics of money and finance because it is the foundation of our livelihood. Our country has become too financially dependant on others and not self-sufficient enough. A significant portion of our population does not understand the value of money until they experience a crisis. If more families were better prepared and informed they wouldn't have to worry about losing their homes because of a job loss. I urge you to please take a little time to understand it, so you can avoid some preventable mistakes.

I feel fortunate that as a young girl, my father was vocal about the cost of borrowing money and pressed the importance of saving. I learned further about how money and interest works, not from high school, but on the job at a savings and loan. I continued my education finally obtaining my bachelor's degree in accounting.

I'm sure that as you read this book you will find there is more to understanding money then simply knowing how to spend it.

I wish you the best.

Reading Tips

Keeping it simple was my mission while writing this book. I feel that this is such an important subject that I do not want any kids to miss out on the basics. I realize that some teens just do not like to read, and these are the ones who probably need this information the most. Therefore, if you are not much for reading, try to at least review the chapter titles, subheadings, and boxed and bulleted information. Of course if you only read the minimum you will miss some valuable information, but you will still gain important and useful knowledge.

I hope this book keeps your attention, but in case you get bored, please don't miss the chapters on interest and the economy. The most important issue relating to finance is knowing how interest effects you when you borrow and save money. The chapter on the economy will give you some simple knowledge to prepare you for your adult life.

Be informed. It will improve your future.

Be Informed

If you were given fifty thousand dollars, what would you do with it? Would you spend it all on a really cool car? Remember, the car will be worth very little in five years, and then where will you be? If you invest the money wisely, then you can make the money grow, and later not only will you be able to buy a cool new car, but also you will still have more money in the bank.

Plus, the comfort level that you gain from the security of a healthy bank account is priceless compared to a fancy new car.

Are you keeping up with the Joneses?

Many people feel lesser of themselves because their neighbors seem to have so much more in the way of material possessions. They may have nicer toys, clothes, cars, a nicer house, and so on. It is sad to think that someone would base their self-worth on material possessions. There is so much more to life than the type of car you drive.

When you hear the cliché "keeping up with the Joneses," it simply means that you are buying stuff just so you can keep up with what your friends and neighbors have. (*The name Jones is an expression for a neighbor's last name.*)

Although material things are nice, I would guess that the average, experienced adult would say that his or her personal relationship with others has given them more enjoyment and happiness than material items. Money can give you financial security, but it can not give you happiness. Financial security is knowing that you will always have enough money to pay your bills and live comfortably. The best part of money is simply the peace of mind that it provides, not the material possessions. Unfortunately many people have it backward and feel the material stuff is the key to their happiness. So they keep looking for pleasure by buying more stuff. The majority of material items will never keep you satisfied because there is always something new to replace it.

You just keep spending money on stuff only to replace it in a year or so with different stuff.

Think about it: the last time you had a really good time, was it because of who you were with or because you just spent a boatload of money on a new cell phone? I guess that cell phone can make you think you look cool. If someone is your real friend, it is probably not because of the car you drive or your fancy cell phone. Do you choose your friends because of the clothes they wear or the house their parents own?

If you happen to come from a family that has very little and always seems to struggle, don't worry, because if you are willing to put in the effort and are careful with your money and personal choices, you can improve your lifestyle.

You can't judge a book by its cover

You have probably heard the saying "you can't judge a book by its cover," and this is especially true when trying to judge the richest kids in school versus the poorest. As it turns out, the kid that you thought came from a family with lots of money could be on the verge of losing their home, when at the same time, the kid who wears cheap clothes and drives a rusted, thirteen-year-old station wagon may never have to worry about money.

Some parents save all their money, and some spend it all. The spenders will have all the nice new stuff so they will look well-off, but don't let your eyes fool you because they could have an empty checking account and some high credit card balances to boot. On the opposite side of the ring are the savers. If they are extreme, you might call them squeaky or tightwad because they will walk around in holey tennis shoes before they will part with a few dollars. They may be the last that you would suspect to have a big bank account, but you won't have to worry about that family losing their house. Hopefully, you have parents somewhere in the middle. Besides, why do you really care what your friend's mom and dad have? Before long, you will be out on your own, and then all that will matter is what *you* do.

For all the little girls whose parents tell them to marry a rich man, make sure that you can financially take care of yourself before you become a dependant of your husband. What will you do if your husband becomes abusive or just decides that he wants a divorce? A plan, a savings account, and an education will give you freedom.

Where are you in the chain of life?

Do you ever feel like your parents just do not understand you or that they can't relate because they are too old? Sometimes parents do not always communicate well, but we were all teenagers at one time, so we do understand, and we just hate to see our kids make mistakes. The purpose of the chart below is for you to visualize how many years are ahead of you to make your own decisions.

Although material things seem important when you are young, you might want to consider the big picture before you start spending all your money. Take a look at the following chart and circle the dot representing your age. Each dot represents one year of life; therefore, each row reflects every ten years. The average life span is around seventy-five for men and eighty for women. How old are you?

Years at home with your parents:

Age 1–10   .   .   .   .

  11–20   .   .   .   . **Age 18** .   .

Years on your own:

Age 21–30   .   .   .   .

  31–40   .   .   .   .

  41–50   .   .   .   .

  51–60   .   .   .   .

  61–70   .   .   .   .

  71–80   .   .   .   .   .   . **. Age 80** .   .

  81–90   .   .   .   .

If you are eighteen then you are at the very beginning of your adulthood and probably have not yet experienced life outside of your parent's home. My point is that you don't know everything yet because you haven't experienced adulthood yet. There are so many things in life that you will have to learn on your own, and managing your money will be one of them. So be informed. Before you discount the advice of your parents and teachers, value their many years of trials and errors and learn from them. Look at the 18 on the chart, and you can see that you have many years ahead to experience life and make your own decisions. It seems that the best way to learn is from your own mistakes, but if you are smart, you can avoid many errors by educating yourself.

While you are living at home, don't get too used to the nice car, house, and clothes that your parents provide you with, because it will come to an end at graduation—unless you're not afraid of work and you can manage your money, and I don't just mean balancing your checkbook, although that is an important start.

And don't waste the years between twenty and forty; they are some of your most important, and they go fast. You will make some of your best memories during these years. Before you start a family, take advantage of your time to build a solid foundation for your future. Once you have children, you will not have as much available time to work, and you will have additional costs.

According to a Web site for MSN Money,[1] older data shows the estimated cost of raising a child, through age seventeen, was up to $249,000. If you divide that over seventeen years, then you could pay around $14,600 per year for your child. Make note that if your child goes to college it will cost more. Nowadays this cost is probably higher.

The sooner you learn how to handle what comes your way, the better off you will be. While you are young, difficult events may seem more traumatic, so before you are ready to give up and throw in the towel, consider this:

I remember being a teenager, and it was pretty tough with all the peer pressure and always wanting to fit in. What my friends thought seemed very important to me then. The clothes that I wore, how I looked, and who my friends were, was a very significant part of my life.

Events that happen during your teenage years are important, but in the grand scheme of things, they will

---

1 Web site: http://moneycentral.msn.com/articles/family/kids/tlkid-scost.asp. Based on a survey by the U.S. Department of Agriculture.

only be important for a few years. When you get out of high school, life will change in many ways. During your teenage years, try not to worry too much about what your friends think. Those years will be gone before you know it. Life is constantly changing, and I can guarantee you that what is important from age ten to twenty will not be as important for the next sixty plus years of your life. If you don't believe me, ask your parent(s) or a respected adult friend.

Remember that everything in life is relative, even age. It is kind of like riding a bike: at first it seems hard, but after a while you get so good you forget how hard it was. Time is the same way: it goes by very slowly as a kid because you have not experienced enough, but after around twenty-one, it begins to fly—really.

Ask Yourself:

*Have you every wanted something just because you thought
it would impress your friends?*

Now is a good time to think about your future.

How to Get What You Want

The sooner you start planning, the quicker you will obtain your goals and dreams, and don't stop dreaming. It is true, for the most part, that you can be anything you want to be as long as you are not afraid of hard work and focus. Here are several steps to assist you in getting what you want:

> ➢ Pay yourself first, and start a savings plan

> ➢ Determine what you want, know the cost, and how you will pay for it

> ➢ Create a budget

> ➢ Stay disciplined

Pay yourself first, and start a savings plan

You should always pay yourself first. That means you need to open a savings account, and discipline yourself to deposit a set amount into it from each paycheck, no matter what. Then forget about it. Before you start spending your money and lining everyone else's pockets, you need to put some into a savings plan for yourself.

You may not be able to afford everything that you want right now, but if you learn to manage your money, your possibilities are endless. You have to plan and be patient. If you want to buy a house you must have money saved. If you keep spending your extra money on shoes and dinner out, you may never have enough cash to afford a decent home.

Saving is a learning process. It takes discipline and sacrifice. Saving birthday and Christmas money is a good start. You can not give into the impulse of buying the newest video game system or cool new cell phone every time you get some cash in your pocket.

I remember a kid in my neighborhood that started out by mowing lawns in the summertime. When he was sixteen, he had saved enough of his lawn mowing money to pay cash for a truck and trailer. A year or so later, he bought a bigger mower and other equipment for larger jobs. He now has a successful lawn care and excavation business. He paid himself first by saving his money, which allowed him to invest in equipment that helped him continue making money.

Reasons to save:

1. Save for a car so you have transportation to your job.

2. Save for higher education in order to attain a better-paying job.

3. Save for unexpected expenses such as your car breaking down.

4. Save to pay your bills in the event that you lose your job.

5. Save for a home so you have no house payment when you retire.

6. Save enough so you can finally retire.

7. Save for vacations and other luxury items.

The list of reasons to save is endless. If you don't have a savings account yet, start one. Trendy styles and cool new toys come and go. Kids and some adults spend most of their money on things that are out of style by the next year. What you bought last year probably, by now, will have no or little value and then it just gets thrown out or given away. For example, you may have a cell phone that you just bought last year and now want to buy a newer high-tech one that costs $250. What will you do with the old one? Doesn't the old phone serve the same purpose as the new one? OK, I'm not saying you should, at sixteen years old, save all your money and never buy another trendy item. In fact, I realize how important it is at sixteen to be fashionable and have some of the latest clothes or toys, but what I hope you get out of this is to be conscious of how you spend. You could probably buy a car at sixteen if you could recover all the money you or your parents spent since you were twelve.

> Before you make any more purchases, always ask yourself if you really need the item or are you just buying it to look good? Furthermore, will you get your use out of it, are you buying it on impulse or could you buy it elsewhere for less?

11

If you do not yet have a car, are you aware that when you buy one you will also have to pay for

- Sales Tax (*depending on the state you live in*)

- Liability Insurance (*at the very least)*

- Personal Property Tax (*due every year)*

- License Plate Renewal Fees

- Inspection Fees

- Gasoline

Of course, the more expensive your car, the more these payments will be. For example, if your car cost $5,000, then depending where you live, you may have to pay sales tax of approximately $380. And remember to drive carefully, without being ticketed or wrecks, so your insurance rates aren't any higher than they already will be. Recently I was told that a new sixteen-years-old female driver will pay about $2,000 per year for full coverage insurance on an older car—that's $166 per month. Male drivers can expect to pay more. If your parents will be footing the bill, you may want to thank them and use this benefit to advance yourself even further.

If you happen to have a parent or parents buying you a car at sixteen and planning on paying for your education, then consider yourself fortunate. Don't take it for granted.

Start saving now so you will obtain you goals sooner. The chapter on retirement has a good example of how your money can grow over time.

Determine what you want, know the cost, and how you will pay for it

If you are like many young men and women, by the time you are twenty-five you probably would like to have your own home, a nice car, money to travel, and nice clothes, or at least some of these things.

It is expected that the average twenty-two-year-old will struggle to pay for a roof over his or her head, food on the table, a car, insurance, clothes, gas, and so on. Therefore, don't place too much pressure on yourself to have it all before you are twenty-five because chances are you won't. Don't be afraid to work and save, and you should do just fine.

Make a list of the top ten things you want to own before you reach thirty. Then put your list in order of importance and finish by eliminating the bottom five. After your list is complete take some time to find out how much each of the items cost. You will then need to figure out how you are going to pay for each item.

Will you save your money so you can pay cash or will you need to borrow? Try to pay cash for smaller items, like stereos and cell phones. You will want to avoid using your credit card to make purchases because the interest rates are so high. Within the chapter on interest is a good example of the cost of using your credit card.

If it is your goal to own a home, make sure you have a realistic price in mind and start saving. When you make large purchases, such as a home, you will probably have to borrow money from the bank. The bank will require you to use some of your own money to buy the home.

This is called a down payment. For example, say you want to buy a home that costs $170,000. Typically, a bank will require that you pay the first 5 to 10 percent for a down payment. Therefore, 5 percent down would be $8,500. You will need at least this much of your own money to get a loan from the bank. Some banks will expect 10 percent ($17,000) or more.

If you have to borrow money to purchase your first car, once that car is paid off continue to put money back each month, so the next time you buy a vehicle you can pay cash and avoid the extra cost of paying interest to the bank.

Getting started is the hardest part for young adults and that is what bank loans are for. Know what you want, recognize the cost, and keep focused on how you will pay for it. These are a few of the steps to get want you want.

Create a budget

A budget is a plan to document your income and expenses to help manage your money. In theory, it is simple, but in reality, it can be difficult if you are not disciplined and stick to the budget.

Remember, when it comes to budgeting, pay yourself first. Creating a budget is pretty simple except you have to be careful to include all your expenses and even add extra for the unexpected.

The average annual wage in the United States, according to the U.S. Census Bureau from 2003,[2] was $37,765, so it is probably around $40,000 now. Although it may take some years after school before you will be

---

2   U.S. Census Bureau, *Statistical Abstract of the United States*, 2006, page 427.

making this much, after taxes, your monthly take home pay may be around $2,400.

Below is a sample monthly budget, first showing your income and then subtracting off your expenses.

Gross Income:

> $3,333.00 Monthly Wages ($40,000/12 months)
> - 500.00 Federal Tax
> - 255.00 Social Security & Medicare Tax
> - <u>150.00</u> State Tax

Net Income:

$2,400.00 Monthly Take Home Pay

Less Monthly Expenses:

- 120.00	Savings (Your Payment) = minimum 5 percent of take home
- 750.00	House Payment or Rent (Cheap)
- 250.00	Car Payment
- 140.00	Insurance for car and house
- 300.00	Food
- 350.00	Utilities (Electric, Phone, Gas, Water, Trash, Cable, Internet)
- 300.00	Health Insurance (portion not paid by employer)
- 50.00	Clothing Allowance
- 100.00	Activities (Movies, Kids Activities, Sports)
- <u>40.00</u>	Emergency, Unexpected expenses (Not taken from savings)
0.00	**Break even**

Once you have created a budget it is important that you stick to it.

Have you ever thought about all the expenses that your parents incur to keep your family going? Ask your mom or dad how much they spend each month on utilities and food. I bet you will be surprised. If you have extra money left over, then put it into your savings account and forget that it is there because the more you save now the sooner you will be financially secure. The 5 percent savings is what some say is a minimum requirement to pay yourself, and you should try to put more in if possible. Especially while you are living at home with your parents and you don't have many expenses, you should be able to save 50 to 70 percent of your income. Save your money now, so you will pay less later. I will explain this in more detail in the chapter on interest.

Stay disciplined

Discipline is key, and you must maintain control to keep it. What I mean is that saving money can be difficult for some people because they want everything now and they don't practice any control. They just spend and buy what they want, without considering the financial consequences. You will have to make small sacrifices, like when you see a really cool new pair of shoes or the latest video game and you just have to tell yourself no. If it is not in your budget, then you can't have it. You should be proud of yourself if you can look past the material items, demonstrate some control, and look at the bigger picture.

You may not want to put in the extra effort, but a little hard work will only make you stronger and more confident with yourself. Think about it: even something as simple as helping your dad or mom do something around the house can give you a sense of accomplishment and pride. On the contrary, if you continually fail to reach your goals, due to lack of control, you may feel less of yourself. As you reach your goals, no matter how big or little, you will feel better about yourself.

> Please do not make the same mistake that many others before you have: living from paycheck to paycheck. It would be sad if your front tooth got knocked out when you tripped in the driveway and you didn't have the $3,000 it would cost to repair it.

Ask Yourself:

How will you get what you want?

While you are at home with your parents and can afford to save more, put at least 70 percent of your money into a savings account. Get as much education that you can, and work hard. When you move out on your own, keep your expenses low, and continue to save as much as possible.

Pay yourself first!

Making Good Choices

<hr/>

I hope this book will give you a head start, before you find yourself over your head with debt. Many choices, even as a teenager, can alter your course of life. The better the choices you make, the better your chances are for success.

Credit reports

Although I recommend saving your money so that you can pay cash for as much as possible, it is necessary for most people to borrow from the bank from time to time. When you open up a credit card or take out a bank loan, you must always make your payments on time. Late payments may be documented with a credit reporting agency, for future lenders to see. Once you are on record as being a late payer, your credit score decreases; as a result you are documented as a bad credit risk, and your chances of getting another loan will be less. If you need to borrow money for a car and have bad credit, you will probably be denied.

Odd as it may seem, if you do not owe anyone because you have always paid cash, your credit score may be lower than a person who charges everything. You need to have some credit to keep your score up unless you plan to pay cash for everything. If you save all your money and are confident that you will never need to borrow money or need a credit card then your credit score will not matter. But in the event that you may need a loan, credit reporting agencies need to observe a good payment history in order to give you a high score.

Things that will lower your credit score are:

- ✓ Too much credit (*applying for too many credit cards*)

- ✓ Slow or late payments

- ✓ Not enough credit (*even if everything you own is paid for*)

Many stores will entice you to open up a credit card account by offering you a discount on your purchase. Remember that too many applications for credit cards and loans will lower your score as well.

Saving versus spending

I remember a conversation with a young friend of mine, and she was talking about a car that her father wanted to give her when she turned sixteen. It was a few years old, and she was concerned that her friends would think she was poor if she was seen driving it. But what she didn't appreciate was that her father was not poor and had more money saved than most, he had few bills, and his house was almost paid for. The reason this was not apparent to her was that her family didn't have a huge house and fancy cars and her parents didn't wear designer clothes.

The other point that she did not consider was that many of the kids she knew who drove nice cars may have had parents with huge mortgages and high credit card debt, along with few dollars saved. If one of the parents lost his or her job or became ill, the family could have their home or cars repossessed by the bank.

When I was about twenty, a friend's grandmother said, "If you drive a fancy car when you're young, you will probably drive a junk car when you're old." As time has gone by, I realize just how right that grandmother was.

In my early twenties, I knew a young man who, at eighteen, inherited $100,000. He went through the money like water. I'm sure at the time he thought he was as cool as he could be with his two brand-new fancy cars, extravagant vacations, clothes, and jewelry. He did not spend any money on his future, like getting a college education or buying a house. By the time he was twenty-two, he was working at a gas station and had spent all of the inheritance. I bet he wishes that he would have made better choices.

You need to know when you should save and when you can spend. As I have said before, you need to pay yourself first. It should be okay to spend if you are staying within your budget and you have planned for unexpected expenses. If you want to buy a new stereo for $2,000 then you need to review your budget to be sure you can do this. If you do not have enough money saved to pay cash, will you have enough to make the monthly payments, without taking from your monthly savings plan? Can you afford a $2,000 stereo without putting yourself in a financially difficult position? If your insurance rates go up or gasoline prices increase again, will you still be able to afford the added monthly payment?

When your money is saved in the proper type of account, at the bank or with an investment firm, you will earn interest on your balance. On the contrary, when you borrow money you will pay interest on the balance of your loan.

As you get older you will need to educate yourself on the many different types of accounts to earn interest and make your money grow. You can put your money into a bank savings account or invest your money into stocks and bonds. Although I do not want to get into detail about the different types of accounts and investments, you do need to be aware that some accounts are insured to prevent you from losing your money and some are high risk that you could lose all of your money. Most banks are insured by the FDIC (Federal Deposit Insurance Corporation) which is about as safe as you can get. Be smart and always ask about the insurance. Some people will invest their money into stocks in the hopes to earn a lot of money fast. Do be careful if you start buying stocks because there is risk that you could lose all of your money. Stocks should only be purchased with money that you will not need to live.

Remember; don't make the same mistake that many others have, living from paycheck to paycheck. It would be sad if you lost your job and consequently lost your home because you didn't have a backup savings account.

Ask Yourself:

What choices can you make now that will increase or decrease your chances of reaching your goals?

Pay your debts on time, and live within your budget. Surround yourself with positive influences because negative people can bring you down. Take advantage of your free education and the variety of classes that it has to offer.

One thing I can tell you is that partying, especially with drugs, will not get you where you want to go.

Interest

Credit cards

Earlier, I mentioned that you should save your money now so that you can pay less later. Let me clarify with a credit card example.

Most of you are probably aware of what a credit card is, but you may not understand how they work. Each time you make a purchase with your credit card, it is just like taking out a loan that you will have to pay back over time. Credit card companies do not lend their money for free, so they will charge you interest on the money you borrow. That interest is the fee, charged by the credit card company and is calculated as a percentage of your balance. Credit card companies love to lend you money because they charge such a high interest rate. They are rolling in *your* dough and laughing all the way to the bank. Although interest rates have been going down, in 2008, credit card rates were averaging around 17 percent, which is extremely high. Beware—around the time you graduate from high school, you become fair game. You will start receiving so many credit card applications in the mail that you are going to need to buy a shredder. It's like being invited for lunch and then finding out you are the main course. When it comes to credit cards, proceed with caution.

A very attractive feature of many credit cards is that you are only required to pay a tiny portion of your balance each month. That sounds nice, but it's the icing on the cake for the bank. For example, the minimum payment required is typically only 1 percent of your balance plus interest and late fees.

If you charged $3,000 on your credit card, 1 percent of that is $30, plus interest calculated on your balance, at a rate of 17 percent: your first monthly payment would be about $70. Seems affordable, but if you only pay the minimum payment until it the card is paid off, it could take around 18 years to pay it off, and by the end, you would have made payments of around of $6,360.00.

Principal Charged	= $3,000.00
Interest Paid	= $3,360.00
Total Payments	= $6,360.00

As you can see, you would end up paying your original charge more than two times over. If you had been able to pay cash, then you would have saved yourself over $3,000 that you paid in interest.

Remember to save first. If your money is in the right kind of savings account, the bank will pay you interest just for keeping your money at their bank.

Mortgage debt

Another example, on a bigger scale, is a home loan. Most people borrow money from the bank when they purchase homes and cars. Again, the bank charges interest on the money you borrow. Therefore, it should make sense that the more money you have saved to put down on your home, the less money you will have to borrow from the bank. Consequently, the less interest you'll have to pay.

Below you will see a comparison of two loans. Let's say that you are buying a house for $175,000. The first loan reflects a down payment of $8,750; therefore, you will borrow $166,250. The second scenario is if you have $35,000 to put down, so you have a loan of $140,000. Both loans have an 8 percent interest rate and are to be paid back over 30 years (standard).

---

8 PERCENT INTEREST PAID TO BANK OVER 30 YEARS

	Principal Borrowed	Monthly Payment	Total Interest Paid after 30 Years
Loan 1	$166,250	$1,219.88	$272,933.61
Loan 2	$140,000	$1,027.27	$229,835.49
DIFFERENCE paid in interest:			$43,098.12
Less Extra Down Payment Paid:			-$26,250.00
		COST:	$16,848.12

You would pay the bank $16,848 more over the life of the loan because you had saved less money for your down payment. Not to mention that your monthly payment will be $192.61 more per month.

So do you see what I mean? If you save more now, you will borrow less and pay the bank less interest. Or just pay cash and not borrow at all. I'm sure there are a lot of things you could buy with an extra $16,848, or maybe just put it into a retirement account.

Think about it: the next time you see a young person driving a junk car, before you criticize him or her, you might consider that he or she has a grand plan. In another ten to fifteen years, his or her house might be paid for, and then he or she will be able to drive nice cars for the rest of his or her life. If you keep spending all your money, you may always struggle.

Another important point to consider is that current home loan rates are only around 5 percent. I do not expect them to stay this low for long. When I started working at a bank at nineteen years old, I think the home loan rates were around 13 percent. Those were the days that you wanted to have money saved in the bank so they would pay you interest. It was not the time to borrow.

Check this out. It would be unfair if I did not show you how incredible the difference is, of the monthly payment and total interest paid, at varying rates. Let's look at the same home loan of $166,250, financed for 30 years, but first at 5 percent, then 8 percent, and finally at 13 percent.

Amount Borrowed	Interest Rate	Monthly Payment	Total Interest Paid after 30 Years
$166,250	5%	$892.47	$155,041.17
$166,250	8%	$1,219.88	$272,933.61
$166,250	13%	$1,839.06	$495,953.27

The difference between what you can buy based on the borrowing rate is quite remarkable. The person who financed a home with the 5 percent interest rate had a whole lot more money in the end, not to mention a great more disposable income each month than the higher rate people. Look at how much difference there is in the monthly payment. If the rates go up to 13 percent again, you will not be able to afford as large of a home because your monthly payment will push you out of that market.

One final point to make note of is that you can save boatloads of money when you make extra payments. Below, you will see a comparison of the same loan, first showing no additional payments, then five extra payments, and finally ten added payments. Using a standard thirty-year home loan at 8 percent interest, you can see the difference in total interest paid is considerable.

If you pay one additional payment at the end of each year for ten years, you will save $58,982.21. Now that is noteworthy.

Amount Borrowed	Additional Payments	Monthly Payment	Total Interest Paid after 30 Years
$166,250	None	$1,219.88	$272,933.61
$166,250	Five	$1,219.88	$233,196.63
$166,250	Ten	$1,219.88	$213,951.40

Interest effect

Unfortunately, we do not have much control over the interest rates. If you have good credit, you can get a thirty-year home loan for around 5 percent, but a few years from now, the rates could very easily be back to 8 percent or more. So just in case, be prepared, and save your money so you will not have to borrow much—or maybe none at all—if you plan well.

If you discipline yourself to save and you have really great parents, maybe they will let you stay at home and save your money until you are thirty, and then you could just pay cash for your home and save yourself about two hundred thousand dollars or more, in bank interest. Just kidding; I don't recommend living with your parents until you are thirty. Besides, your parents may send me hate mail. Hopefully you get the point. Paying interest on credit cards and bank loans is the expensive cost of not saving your own money.

The credit card and home loan examples I used above were fixed rate loans. A fixed rate is a percentage which will not change throughout the term of the loan. Be very careful if you are ever offered a variable rate loan. Variable rate loans can increase the percentage during the term of the loan and they usually do. They are very attractive because they offer a lower rate to start, but then the rate almost always increases. They should only be used in limited, short-term situations.

When I was around ten years old, I remember my mother crying because she was concerned that the bank might foreclose (take back) on our home. At that time, I had just about enough money in my savings account to make one house payment, so I offered it to my mom. Of course she never took my savings, and soon after, everything worked out. But that is a position I hope no one ever has to endure. Back then, my parents (mom and bonus dad) had a variable rate business loan that went from 8 percent to 21 percent, and as you have seen in the above examples, a jump in interest like that can cause extreme hardship.

I hope life is everything you dream of. With a good plan, your dreams can come true. Remember that it is not important what your parents have, because in only a few short years, you will be looking at what you have, and what your parents have won't be an issue anymore. Therefore, spend your dollars wisely.

Computing simple interest is a very easy and basic math skill to learn, and it is useful in everyday life. Therefore, for the group of you who do not know how to calculate a percentage, information has been provided in the Basic Math section at the end of the book. It's easier than you think, and it is helpful in everyday life.

Ask Yourself:

Would you rather pay interest to the bank or have the bank pay you?

When you borrow money, always ask how much interest you will pay over the life of the loan.

Retirement

I will try to keep this chapter simple, because the idea of retirement may be a little hard to relate to when you're still a teenager. Just keep these thoughts in mind:

If you put away $2,000 each year with an investment that earns 8 percent, starting at

* Age 25 until age 65, the ending value will be about $559,500.
* Age 40 until age 65, the ending value will be about $157,900.

That is a sizeable difference. The extra $401,600 at retirement would come in handy and should be worth the effort of starting early.

A retirement plan is an account designed for you to have income when you retire. There are three primary sources for retirement income:

➢ Employer Plans

➢ Personal Retirement Savings

➢ Social Security

Even if your job offers you an employer plan, it may still be a good idea to build your own personal retirement plan. There have been many people who lost their company pensions or employer retirement plans because of business closings and mismanagement. You never know, so you should establish your own retirement plan. There are different types of individual or personal retirement plans and a good place to find them is your local bank or investment broker. If you have paid in, social security will provide income at retirement, but it is typically only enough for the bare minimum.

Just in case you are unaware of what social security is, it is a tax of 7.65 percent taken from every paycheck, but there is an annual limit. This money is then put into a federal program designed to provide income for workers and their families who are too old, ill, or disabled to work, or it pays out to the family of individuals who have suffered from early death. It has developed into a plan to help most people supplement their income at retirement. At present, you must be at least sixty-two years old to begin drawing social security. The eligible age keeps increasing because people are living longer and the population of retirees is increasing. I think that I will be eligible to draw from social security at around seventy, and the age is likely going to be much older for your generation—if social security will even be available. By the time you are ready for retirement, social security may not provide enough to live on. And you may even want to quit your job before age seventy. Therefore, you will need an additional plan.

If you are self-employed, you will be responsible for paying into social security on your own. At retirement age, if you have not paid into social security or do not have an employer or personal retirement plan, then you will have no income, so you will not be able to quit working.

It would be a tragedy if you ended up living on the streets because you had no plan and no income.

Ask Yourself:

How would you like to live during your retirement years?

You need to plan, and the earlier you start, the better off you will be.

Economy

History

The drop in our economy is nothing new. Unfortunately, times have been good for so long that people forgot the first rule: pay yourself first. Our economy is constantly changing and always has, so don't assume that it will stay the same. You need to be prepared and have a backup savings account. It cannot be our government's duty to bail everyone out of trouble every time a disaster occurs, whether it is natural or financial.

We have little or no control over factors such as interest rates, gasoline prices, food prices, utilities rates, health insurance costs, and other prices that affect our wallets. However, one thing that we do have control over is our own fortune.

Your future

There are many reasons why the economy is in trouble right now. As a teenager, you may be wondering why this should be important to you. It will not be long until you are out of school, and it will be your turn to start looking for a job. The higher the unemployment rate, the harder it will be to compete for a good job. In other words, the more people who are unemployed and looking for employment, the more competition there will be for you to find a job. The way things are going, your generation may have to start working at a lower standard of income. Money is tight, and families are not out buying houses and cars, going out to dinner, vacationing, or buying toys. If people are not spending money, then industries struggle, and consequently, unemployment is higher. Employers are making cut backs and some employees are offering to cut back hours and lower their hourly rate to keep their jobs.

American families and businesses have become spoiled, and it is catching up with us. It has been the trend to work less and get paid more, but I think we have pushed this concept past the limit. It seems we will now have to work more and get paid less. Our businesses and individuals need to band together, become more productive, and cut inefficiencies where we can. We should put in an honest days work for an honest days pay.

When it comes to working, always be smart, honest, reliable, hardworking, and easy to get along with. When work slows down and employers have to make job cuts, the first to go will probably be the employee that is not reliable or is difficult to work with. Unfortunately, though, even some of the good ones get laid off.

We should all take a little more responsibility for our own actions. If you do a little preparing, hopefully your generation will be a lot smarter and you will never have to worry about losing your house to the bank, losing your job, or feeding your children. This is a great country full of generous and honest people; we just need to plan better.

Lessons learned

With the condition of the economy, it has never been more apparent that one of our biggest failures is the simple teaching of money management. We need to inform our teenagers and teach independence, not dependence. Times are really tough, and people are losing their jobs. What complicates this further is the fact that many people are not prepared. We are way too dependant on our next paycheck, our credit cards, and the government. With too many dependants, our country will continue on a downhill slide.

A good goal to work toward is to save enough cash equal to two years salary. I have heard anywhere from six months to two years. Although it will take some time to obtain this goal, remember that the more saved the better. And your savings account should not be confused with your retirement money.

I have seen businesses and families go broke because they have too much debt, and as soon as the economy slows, they can't keep up. When your income drops but your expenses stay the same, you will incur a problem. Be sure you can afford your monthly payments even in the worst case scenario. Our economy in 2004, 2005, and 2006 was booming, and there was a lot of money being made. People were out buying more equipment, bigger homes, new cars, boats, expensive toys for the kids, and dinner out a few times a week. The problem is that they borrowed too much and didn't put enough in savings to hold them over and to help pay the mortgage, car payments, and credit card debt in case of an emergency. Now work is hard to find.

If you have to wait each month to pay your bills until you receive your paycheck—in other words, living from paycheck to paycheck—chances are good that you will encounter financial hardship. As soon as you start working, even as a teenager, you should start putting a portion of every paycheck into your savings because you never know when you may incur an unexpected emergency such as a car repair, tooth repair, or lost job.

Remember to make a budget. Many people forget to plan ahead, so when the tax and insurance bills show up or the car breaks down or the kids need new tennis shoes, they may find themselves a bit short on money. Cable, Internet, cell phones, and dinner out are all luxury items that can be cut out if money is tight. You really can live without luxury items—it is easier than you think. Life was still fun before cable, Internet, and cell phones.

Banks are taking the blame for much of the economic crisis now, but inflation was growing out of sight before the banking problems started. Inflation is an unstable rise in price levels. Prices for gasoline, homes, insurance, food, technology, and just about every other commodity was going up at a rate so fast that it was not a surprise that something was going to give. Now it is giving. Companies are struggling to pay high wages, and families can't afford their bank loans. It is unfortunate that companies like the gas, insurance, and home building industry, along with most every other business, have raised rates so much over the past four to five years that collectively it has stretched our wallets too far and has proved to be too much. Lesson learned. Be prepared for the unexpected.

Ask Yourself:

Will you be prepared if you lose your job?

Ultimately we should be responsible for our own actions. Be honest. When times are tough, you may have to work harder.

Other Motherly Concerns

This chapter has nothing to do with finances. As a mother I am simply passing on a few tips.

Try to keep things in perspective when life gets tough. Sometimes you just have to take a breath, let some time go by, let emotions cool off, and things will work out.

Drugs

Don't do drugs. Don't be afraid to say NO, and don't let some pothead pressure you by calling you chicken. Let them screw up their own lives, but keep yourself out of it. Drugs are a certain way to ruin your life before you even get started. Drugs can be so addicting that after one try you could be hooked for the rest of your life. Addicts will sell anything to get drugs because their bodies are physically dependant on them. I have seen people turn over all of their money, week after week, year after year, for drugs. In the end, you could become a broken down old person with nothing to your name—not even a real friend.

Relationships

When it is time for you to pick a boyfriend or girlfriend, please take your time and try to find someone who has similar interests as you. Although, as most everyone does, you will have to learn from your own mistakes. Try and get to know someone before you give them your heart.

It is easy to become attracted to someone at first sight, but looks alone will not keep a relationship together. There are so many variables to making a relationship work. For example, there may be two people who are attracted to each other and have some of the same friends, so they decide to date and become emotionally tied to each other early in their relationship. They enjoy hanging out with their friends, and they appear to be a good match. One of them is really neat and tidy, careful with his or her finances, easygoing, and enjoys being around people. The other partner is a slob, spends money carelessly, and only likes to be around some people and is very critical of others. As time goes by, their relationship becomes strained because one of them feels like the other is not pulling his or her weight with paying for dates or keeping their appearance nice. Then the other person feels like he or she is being nagged about helping, so they fight more and eventually break up.

Many marriages have failed because of money issues, alcohol (particularly, drinking too much), personal hygiene, cleanliness, social skills, lack of communication, differences in raising children, and many other reasons. There are so many challenges for couples to face. The more you get to know your partner early, before you give your heart away, the better chances your relationship will have to survive. Of course, the flip side is that if you find someone and after a few months of dating you realize that you aren't right for each other, you have to be strong enough to break off the relationship respectfully.

Friendships and sharing

Try to always be considerate of others, and do your best to surround yourself with nice people as well. Share and be giving, but be careful of takers. Some people, unfortunately, are better at taking than giving. Many of us want to be able to give, but please give only what you can afford. Don't give away your retirement, and your savings is your retirement no matter how you look at it.

Sometimes we feel down and look at all the negative aspects in life, but if you look around, you will see during holidays, special events, or tragic times that people want to give whatever they can, even if that means having less for themselves. We live in a great country because of all the generous people who donate so much of their time and money.

There are so many types of people that you will experience along life's path, and as long as people are considerate, then it shouldn't matter if they are a different color or nationality or if they have different interests than you.

The end

Be smart, be informed, and be prepared in everything you do. Use the experiences of others so you can avoid a few pitfalls.

Life is full of choices. Sometimes the right choice is the harder one, but chances are you will be happier in the end.

I wish you all of life's best, sincerely.

Ask Yourself

In the end, what do you think will matter?

You have to decide what is more important to you:
looking cool or being successful?

Basic Math

I strongly recommend that everyone take additional classes on finance and money. Most high schools and community colleges have some great classes.

Percentages

If you go to the store and see a sign that says Sale 10 percent Off, could you figure the discount in your head? It can be as simple as moving a decimal place. For each 10 percent you just move the decimal place over to the left one spot. For example, if you move the decimal over one spot to the left on $50.00 then you would have $5.00, so 10 percent of 50 is 5.

If the original cost of the item you are looking at is $50.00 and we know that 10 percent is $5.00, then 20 percent would be twice as much. Five plus five is ten. So, 20 percent of $50.00 is $10.00. Further, 25 percent is twice plus half, or $5.00 plus $5.00 plus half, $2.50, which equals $12.50.

Recap:
$50.00 Original Cost

10% = $5.00
20% = $10.00
25% = $12.50

Like everything else, once you practice it enough, it becomes easy.